The Story of the
Matthew 1
Luke 9:10–

GW00992827

A MEAL FOR MANY

Written by Erik J. Rottmann

Illustrated by
Pat Paris

Arch® Books, Copyright ©2003 Concordia Publishing House. 3558 S. Jefferson Avenue, St. Louis, MO 63118-3968. Manufactured Colombia. All rights reserved. No part of this publication may be reproduced, stored in a retrieval system, or transmitted, in any form or by any means, electronic, mechanical, photocopying, recording, or otherwise, without the prior written permission of Concordia Publishing House.

One springtime day in Galilee
Our Lord got in a boat.
He sailed far out across the sea
To find someplace remote.

But when His boat hit land again
To find that rest so rare,
The people ran along the shore.
They rushed to meet Him there.

Five thousand men all met the Lord.
They brought their loved ones, too.
When Jesus saw them gathered there,
He knew just what to do:

He welcomed every boy and girl,
Each mother and each dad;
He gave the sick His healing touch;
His presence made them glad.

But when the time for supper came
There was no bread or meat.
So Jesus' friends all said to Him,
"There's nothing here to eat!"

"Tell all these people, 'Go away!'
We can't feed them tonight.
Not even eight months worth of pay
Would give each one a bite!"

Then Simon's brother, Andrew, said,
"Lord, if this will do,
Here is a boy who has some food
He'd like to give to You."

The boy gave Jesus two small fish
And five small loaves of bread.
Lord Jesus gladly took the gift
Then upward raised His head.

And when He gave His Father thanks,
He broke the bread and fish.
His friends gave supper to the crowd.
They said, "Eat all you wish."

Twelve baskets full of bread remained
When everyone was done.
His friends each gathered up the food.
They wasted not a crumb!

How happy must have been that boy
Who gave the Lord his best!
For even though the gift was small,
Lord Jesus did the rest.

God loves the gifts His people bring
Of money, time, or deeds.
He gladly puts them into use
To serve His people's needs.

So give to God your very best,
And give your gifts with joy.
He welcomes every act of faith
Just as He did the boy's!

Yet even more than what we give,
Lord Jesus gave to us.
He gave His very dearest gift
In death upon a cross.

But when they laid Him in the tomb
Lord Jesus was not through.
His resurrection is a gift:
Lord Jesus rose for you!

And yet another gift remains
For Christians large and small:
Christ shall return and we shall live
In resurrection all!

Dear Parents,

Jesus' miracle of feeding 5,000 illustrates the great love and compassion our Lord has for us: "When Jesus landed and saw a large crowd, He had compassion on them, because they were like sheep without a shepherd" (Mark 6:34). This miracle also shows the response of faith: "Here is a boy with five small barley loaves and two small fish" (John 6:9). Such giving not only imitates our Lord's lavish generosity toward us, but finds its power and its willingness in His gifts!

Emphasize for your children that this story focuses on Jesus, the Giver of gifts. He not only gives the great spiritual gifts of forgiveness and eternal life, but He gives gifts to support our earthly bodies and lives. Discuss with your children the many gifts that God gives. Look for ideas in the *Small Catechism*, especially the explanations to the three articles of the Apostles' Creed. Use the example of the boy in this story to talk about different ways Christians respond to God's gifts.

Finally, emphasize for them the greatest gift of all time: the gift of salvation that is now theirs and yours through Jesus Christ's crucifixion and resurrection.

The Author